SHERLOCK
HOLMES
FOR LAWYERS

CECIL C. KUHNE III

SHERLOCK HOLMES
FOR LAWYERS

100 CLUES FOR LITIGATORS FROM THE MASTER DETECTIVE

AMERICAN BAR ASSOCIATION
**Defending Liberty
Pursuing Justice**

Cover design by Kelly Book/ABA Publishing.
Interior design by Betsy Kulak/ABA Publishing.

The materials contained herein represent the opinions of the authors and/or the editors, and should not be construed to be the views or opinions of the law firms or companies with whom such persons are in partnership with, associated with, or employed by, nor of the American Bar Association unless adopted pursuant to the bylaws of the Association.

Nothing contained in this book is to be considered as the rendering of legal advice for specific cases, and readers are responsible for obtaining such advice from their own legal counsel. This book is intended for educational and informational purposes only.

Front cover photo: James H. Lane, Brady's National Photographic Portrait Galleries, photographer

Printed in the United States of America.

20 19 18 17 16   5 4 3 2 1

Library of Congress Cataloging-in-Publication Data

Names: Kuhne, Cecil C., III, 1952– compiler.
  Title: Sherlock Holmes for lawyers : 100 clues for litigators from the master detective / Cecil C. Kuhne III.
  Description: Chicago, Illinois : American Bar Association, 2015.
  Identifiers: LCCN 2015043389 (print) | LCCN 2015044605 (ebook) |
ISBN 9781634251976 (softcover : alk. paper) | ISBN 9781634251983 ()
  Subjects: LCSH: Trial practice—Quotations, maxims, etc. | Holmes, Sherlock—Quotations. |
Doyle, Arthur Conan, 1859–1930—Quotations.
  Classification: LCC K2250 .K84 2015 (print) | LCC K2250 (ebook) | DDC
  347/.0504—dc23
LC record available at http://lccn.loc.gov/2015043389

Discounts are available for books ordered in bulk. Special consideration is given to state bars, CLE programs, and other bar-related organizations. Inquire at Book Publishing, ABA Publishing, American Bar Association, 321 N. Clark Street, Chicago, Illinois 60654-7598.

www.ShopABA.org

"Excellent!" I cried.
"Elementary," said he.

———

"The Crooked Man," *The Memoirs of Sherlock Holmes* (1894)

Introduction

Sherlock Holmes, the iconic fictional English detective that he was, had a lot to teach modern-day lawyers about logical reasoning and forensic science. The popular and well-beloved creation of the Scottish author and physician Sir Arthur Conan Doyle, Sherlock Holmes was an immediate success after he first appeared in print in 1887. Doyle went on to write four novels and 56 short stories about the intellectual exploits of Holmes, and almost all of them were narrated by the renowned and amiable Dr. Watson.

Of course, Doyle was a prolific writer who penned many other novels, plays, and poems. I've included entries from several of these other works, as well. Perhaps readers will be encouraged to explore Doyle's other writings. My hope is that you will find this collection of wit and wisdom to be interesting, illuminating, and yes, even . . . elementary.

— *Clue 1* —

I consider that a man's brain originally is like a little empty attic, and you have to stock it with such furniture as you choose. A fool takes in all the lumber of every sort that he comes across, so that the knowledge which might be useful to him gets crowded out, or at best is jumbled up with a lot of other things, so that he has a difficulty in laying his hands upon it. Now the skillful workman is very careful indeed as to what he takes into his brain-attic.

—*A Study in Scarlet* (1887)

What it means: *The finite mind tends to overfill with worthless details.*

How to use it: *This suggestion is critical when presenting your case to judge or jury: Keep matters as clear and simple as possible so that the point of your argument is not lost in the deep, dark morass.*

Nothing clears up a case so much as stating it to another person.

—"Silver Blaze," *The Memoirs of Sherlock Holmes* (1893)

What it means: *Clear thought results from verbally expressing an idea.*

How to use it: *This is an invaluable piece of advice for litigators: Never make a legal argument to a judge or jury until it has been thoroughly vetted by explaining it to others (preferably those who are not lawyers).*

— Clue 3 —

Life is infinitely stranger than anything which the mind of man could invent. We would not dare to conceive the things which are really mere commonplaces of existence. If we could fly out of that window hand in hand, hover over this great city, gently remove the roofs, and peep in at the queer things which are going on, the strange coincidences, the plannings, the cross-purposes, the wonderful chains of events, working through generations, and leading to the most outré results, it would make all fiction with its conventionalities and foreseen conclusions most stale and unprofitable.

—"A Case of Identity," *The Adventures of Sherlock Holmes* (1892)

What it means: *The complexities of human behavior cannot be forced into a tidy box.*

How to use it: *You must instruct the judge or jury that, in assessing the case before them, they should disregard all preconceived notions and let the facts—strange as they may seem—come to light.*

One should always look for a possible alternative, and provide against it.

—"The Adventure of Black Peter,"
The Return of Sherlock Holmes (1905)

What it means: *Anticipate everything.*

How to use it: *When preparing a case for trial, mediation, or arbitration, you can never be too cautious in trying to envision what pitfalls may lie ahead—and then crafting the appropriate response.*

— *Clue 5* —

[Hopkins:] "There were no footmarks."

[Holmes:] "Meaning that you saw none?"

[Hopkins] "I assure you, sir, that there were none."

[Holmes:] "My good Hopkins, I have investigated many crimes, but I have never yet seen one which was committed by a flying creature. As long as the criminal remains upon two legs so long must there be some indentation, some abrasion, some trifling displacement which can be detected by the scientific searcher."

—"The Adventure of Black Peter,"
The Return of Sherlock Holmes (1905)

What it means: *Every movement leaves an impression.*

How to use it: *When investigating a case, you should examine it closely for physical explanations until you find the most reasonable one. The traces are there if you look hard enough.*

— Clue 6 —

It is a tangled skein, you understand, and I am looking for a loose end.

—"Adventure of the Blanched Soldier,"
The Case-Book of Sherlock Holmes (1926)

What it means: *Human events are infinitely complex.*

How to use it: *In assessing a complicated legal situation, you must search for a lead—any lead—pointing the way to the truth that lies beneath the jumbled facts. The process can be tedious but is absolutely necessary.*

— *Clue 7* —

I said that he was my superior in observation and deduction. If the art of the detective began and ended in reasoning from an armchair, my brother would be the greatest criminal agent that ever lived. But he has no ambition and no energy. He will not even go out of his way to verify his own solutions, and would rather be considered wrong than take the trouble to prove himself right.

—"The Greek Interpreter," *The Memoirs of Sherlock Holmes* (1893)

What it means: *Hard work is the key to success.*

How to use it: *Wearing out the shoe leather and burning the midnight oil allows an attorney to conquer his less ambitious adversaries, even those considered more intelligent and better educated.*

— *Clue 8* —

They were admirable things for the observer—excellent for drawing the veil from men's motives and actions. But for the trained reasoner to admit such intrusions into his own delicate and finely adjusted temperament was to introduce a distracting factor which might throw a doubt upon all his mental results. Grit in a sensitive instrument, or a crack in one of his own high-power lenses, would not be more disturbing than a strong emotion in a nature such as his.

—"A Scandal in Bohemia," *The Adventures of Sherlock Holmes* (1892)

What it means: *Stay completely detached.*

How to use it: *You must be careful not to let your prejudices interfere with your duty to the client and the court. Even the slightest deviation from a rational approach can mar your integrity.*

— *Clue 9* —

There is nothing more deceptive than an obvious fact.

—"The Boscombe Valley Mystery,"
The Adventures of Sherlock Holmes (1892)

What it means: *Things are almost never as they first appear.*

How to use it: *The situation before you may seem straightforward at first, but the truth is often otherwise. Look for alternatives that are not readily apparent—reality may lie there.*

— *Clue 10* —

It has long been an axiom of mine that the little things are infinitely the most important.

—"A Case of Identity," *The Adventures of Sherlock Holmes* (1892)

What it means: *Mastering details is of utmost importance.*

How to use it: *You should search for the minute and the less obvious as you prepare your case for trial. The big themes will take care of themselves.*

— *Clue 11* —

It is a capital mistake to theorize before one has data. Insensibly one begins to twist facts to suit theories, instead of theories to suit facts.

—"A Scandal in Bohemia," *The Adventures of Sherlock Holmes* (1892)

What it means: *Accumulate the facts before analyzing the case.*

How to use it: *Preconceived notions will distort your analysis. Accuracy depends upon analyzing the proven facts.*

— *Clue 12* —

To begin at the beginning.

—*A Study in Scarlet* (1887)

What it means: *Chronology is critical.*

How to use it: *You should prepare a timeline so that the decision makers can easily comprehend the situation at hand. Only then can they order the events in such a way that allows clear analysis.*

— *Clue 13* —

His ignorance was as remarkable as his knowledge.

—*A Study in Scarlet* (1887)

What it means: *A person's intelligence, however substantial, can sometimes be narrow and therefore distorted.*

How to use it: *As a trial lawyer, you must be aware that the knowledge of a witness or expert may not extend beyond her particular area of expertise.*

— Clue 14 —

Depend upon it, there is nothing so unnatural as the commonplace.

—"A Case of Identity," *The Adventures of Sherlock Holmes* (1892)

What it means: *Expect the unexpected.*

How to use it: *Once a trial lawyer begins to assume an outcome, he blinds himself to the reality of what really happened. You must remember that things are rarely as they first appear.*

— *Clue 15* —

My name is Sherlock Holmes. It is my business to know what other people don't know.

—"The Adventure of the Blue Carbuncle,"
The Adventures of Sherlock Holmes (1892)

What it means: *Knowledge is power.*

How to use it: *Resolve to be the most thorough litigator you can be, no matter how arduous the task. As a result, you will achieve extraordinary success.*

— *Clue 16* —

It is a pity he did not write in pencil. As you have no doubt frequently observed, the impression usually goes through—a fact which has dissolved many a happy marriage.

—"The Adventure of the Missing Three-Quarter,"
The Return of Sherlock Holmes (1905)

What it means: *Truth is almost always revealed eventually.*

How to use it: *When preparing a case for trial, diligently follow faint trails. They will often lead to revelations never before imagined.*

— *Clue 17* —

The affair seems absurdly trifling, and yet I dare call nothing trivial when I reflect that some of my most classic cases have had the least promising commencement. You will remember, Watson, how the dreadful business of the Abernetty family was first brought to my notice by the depth which the parsley had sunk into the butter upon a hot day.

—"The Adventure of the Six Napoleons,"
The Return of Sherlock Holmes (1905)

What it means: *Persist in the face of adversity.*

How to use it: *An attorney must never give up as she defends her client. Some of the most difficult cases are suddenly (and surprisingly) turned around by small events.*

— *Clue 18* —

All my instincts are one way, and all the facts are the other, and I much fear that British juries have not yet attained that pitch of intelligence when they will give the preference to my theories over Lestrade's facts.

—"The Adventure of the Norwood Builder,"
The Return of Sherlock Holmes (1905)

What it means: *Facts are everything.*

How to use it: *When presenting a case to a jury, it is important to remember that the story line is more persuasive than a clever legal theory.*

— *Clue 19* —

It is of the first importance not to allow your judgment to be biased by personal qualities. A client is to me a mere unit—a factor in a problem.

—*The Sign of the Four* (1890)

What it means: *Keep your client relations impartial.*

How to use it: *An attorney must approach the case with a clinical view, and he should never let a personal relationship with the client cloud his professional judgment.*

— *Clue 20* —

There is nothing like first-hand evidence.

—*A Study in Scarlet* (1887)

What it means: *Circumstantial evidence has its limitations.*

How to use it: *Whenever possible, you should gather information that has been directly observed. These verifiable facts are almost always more reliable than those facts that are inferred.*

— *Clue 21* —

The world is full of obvious things which nobody by any chance ever observes.

—*The Hound of the Baskervilles* (1902)

What it means: *Look around!*

How to use it: *An attorney often becomes numb to the circumstances that surround the case. It is important to maintain a fresh outlook for these revelations.*

— *Clue 22* —

You see, but you do not observe. The distinction is clear.

—"A Scandal in Bohemia,"
The Adventures of Sherlock Holmes (1892)

What it means: *Knowledge is not necessarily understanding.*

How to use it: *A trial lawyer must delve deep into the facts and the law of the case in order to truly comprehend it.*

— *Clue 23* —

I never guess. It is a shocking habit—destructive to the logical faculty.

—*The Sign of the Four* (1890)

What it means: *Avoid conjecture.*

How to use it: *When evaluating a case, you must stick to tangible and verifiable evidence. Guesswork is insufficient to withstand the stresses of judicial inquiry.*

23

— *Clue 24* —

You know my method. It is founded upon the observation of trifles.

—"The Boscombe Valley Mystery,"
The Adventures of Sherlock Holmes (1892)

What it means: *No detail is too small.*

How to use it: *A litigator, in her quest for excellence, must be vigorous in her efforts to ferret out the facts of the case and the law on the books. Perfection comes no other way.*

— Clue 25 —

[Gregory:] "Is there any point to which you would wish to draw my attention?"

[Holmes:] "To the curious incident of the dog in the night-time."

[Gregory] "The dog did nothing in the night-time."

[Holmes] "That was the curious incident," remarked Sherlock Holmes.

—"Silver Blaze," *The Memoirs of Sherlock Holmes* (1893)

What it means: *Omission counts as much as commission.*

How to use it: *In his search for a winning strategy, a lawyer should look as carefully for the facts that are missing as those that readily present themselves. To do otherwise omits much that is important.*

— *Clue 26* —

How often have I said to you that when you have eliminated the impossible, whatever remains, however improbable, must be the truth?

—*The Sign of the Four* (1890)

What it means: *Never underestimate the power of elimination.*

How to use it: *In a confused situation—where the answer is not readily apparent—it may be necessary to select the most probable cause by discarding weaker ones.*

— Clue 27 —

"Data! Data! Data!" he [Holmes] cried impatiently. "I can't make bricks without clay."

—"The Adventure of the Copper Beeches,"
The Adventures of Sherlock Holmes (1892)

What it means: *Substance is everything.*

How to use it: *Solid cases are never made of thin air, so you must pay careful attention to the proof and supporting law that are essential to a sturdy foundation.*

— *Clue 28* —

There is nothing new under the sun. It has all been done before.

—*A Study in Scarlet* (1887)

What it means: *Don't reinvent the wheel.*

How to use it: *Console yourself with the thought that you are not the first one to face the situation before you, and, as a result, you will not be intimidated by the task ahead.*

— *Clue 29* —

I ought to know by this time that when a fact appears to be opposed to a long train of deductions it invariably proves to be capable of bearing some other interpretation.

—*A Study in Scarlet* (1887)

What it means: *Pay close attention to analytical weaknesses.*

How to use it: *It is tempting to ignore the shaky logic in your case, but you run a big risk in doing so. The frailty of a weak argument will be exposed in due time, and a better course lies elsewhere.*

— *Clue 30* —

I never make exceptions. An exception disproves the rule.

—*The Sign of the Four* (1890)

What it means: *Stick to your plan.*

How to use it: *A litigator has to be resolute in her approach to the case. After considering all the alternatives, she must remain steadfast in her chosen course of action.*

— *Clue 31* —

The emotional qualities are antagonistic to clear reasoning.

—*The Sign of the Four* (1890)

What it means: *Think rationally.*

How to use it: *A trial lawyer must convince the jury members to discard their emotional predilections. The cool light of objectivity—you must reiterate to them—is far better for achieving justice.*

— *Clue 32* —

Having gathered these facts, Watson, I smoked several pipes over them, trying to separate those which were crucial from others which were merely incidental.

—"The Adventure of the Crooked Man,"
The Memoirs of Sherlock Holmes (1893)

What it means: *Take time for deep contemplation.*

How to use it: *Sifting the relevant from the irrelevant requires a great deal of effort and patience, and there are no shortcuts through the laborious process.*

— *Clue 33* —

I confess that I have been blind as a mole, but it is better to learn wisdom late than never to learn it at all.

—"The Man with the Twisted Lip,"
The Adventures of Sherlock Holmes (1892)

What it means: Inspiration often comes later.

How to use it: A litigator must never give up his search for the best solution to a legal problem. The path can be elusive, but you must remain patient and diligent.

— *Clue 34* —

It is my belief, Watson, founded upon my experience, that the lowest and vilest alleys in London do not present a more dreadful record of sin than does the smiling and beautiful countryside.

—"The Adventure of the Copper Beeches,"
The Adventures of Sherlock Holmes (1892)

What it means: *You can't tell a book by its cover.*

How to use it: *What first appears to be lovely and dignified is often a façade. The trial lawyer must instead concern himself with reality.*

— Clue 35 —

I shall just have time to tell you the facts of the case before we get to Lee. It seems absurdly simple, and yet, somehow I can get nothing to go upon. There's plenty of thread, no doubt, but I can't get the end of it into my hand.

—"The Man with the Twisted Lip,"
The Adventures of Sherlock Holmes (1892)

What it means: *The simple is often complicated.*

How to use it: *As a trial lawyer, you must not be convinced of what appears to be a straightforward situation until you have proven it to be such.*

The authorities are excellent at amassing facts, though they do not always use them to advantage.

—"The Naval Treaty," *The Memoirs of Sherlock Holmes* (1893)

What it means: *Government power has its limits.*

How to use it: *When dealing with the authorities, you must remember that they often fail to effectively utilize their substantial resources. Parlay this limitation to your client's advantage.*

— *Clue 37* —

Why should you, for a mere passing pleasure, risk the loss of those great powers with which you have been endowed?

—*The Sign of the Four* (1890)

What it means: *A reputation is exceedingly fragile.*

How to use it: *Guard your professional achievements zealously by maintaining your integrity, your honesty, and your diligence. Nothing is worth their loss.*

— *Clue 38* —

However, I guess your time is of value, and we did not meet to talk about the cut of my socks.

—"The Adventure of the Mazarin Stone,"
The Case-Book of Sherlock Holmes (1921)

What it means: *Time is money.*

How to use it: *Get to the bottom of the case as quickly and efficiently as you can for the sake of your client—and for the judge and jury who will decide it.*

— Clue 39 —

Education never ends, Watson. It is a series of lessons, with the greatest for the last.

—"The Adventure of the Red Circle," *His Last Bow* (1911)

What it means: *Learning is a continual process.*

How to use it: *The challenge of practicing law rests upon the recognition that perfection is never achieved. With the benefit of hindsight, you could have always done a better job, and you must learn from previous experience.*

— *Clue 40* —

What you do in this world is a matter of no consequence. The question is what can you make people believe you have done.

—*A Study in Scarlet* (1887)

What it means: *Appearance is reality.*

How to use it: *Rightly or wrongly, one's reputation is built on the perceptions of others, so your image must be carefully guarded. You can be the best lawyer in the world, but if no one knows, it makes little difference.*

— *Clue 41* —

I am an omnivorous reader with a strangely retentive memory for trifles.

—"The Adventure of the Lion's Mane,"
The Case-Book of Sherlock Holmes (1926)

What it means: *Read widely and deeply.*

How to use it: *To adequately prepare a case, you must amass copious amounts of information and then delve into its minute details. Only then can you serve as an effective advocate.*

— *Clue 42* —

There are always some lunatics about. It would be a dull world without them.

—"The Adventure of the Three Gables,"
The Case-Book of Sherlock Holmes (1926)

What it means: *Revel in the world's diversity.*

How to use it: *As a trial lawyer, you should never be surprised when you encounter strange and unusual people. Take them in stride, and enjoy the challenges they bring.*

— *Clue 43* —

One drawback of an active mind is that we can always conceive alternate explanations which would make our scent a false one.

—"The Problem of Thor Bridge,"
The Case-Book of Sherlock Holmes (1927)

What it means: *Avoid overthinking.*

How to use it: *Intelligence—with its great analytical possibilities—often hinders one from finding a prompt and practical solution to the problem, and this can prove detrimental to the client.*

— Clue 44 —

"To a great mind, nothing is little," remarked Holmes, sententiously.

—*A Study in Scarlet* (1887)

44

What it means: *Consider all the circumstances.*

How to use it: *Legal solutions are like a puzzle, with the small pieces being just as important as the large ones in the picture that finally emerges.*

— *Clue 45* —

The unexpected has happened so continually in my life that it has ceased to deserve the name.

—*The Stark Munro Letters* (1895)

What it means: *Expect the unexpected.*

How to use it: *An attorney should never be surprised by unusual developments in the case. She must come to revel in them and the hurdles they inevitably pose.*

Crime is common. Logic is rare. Therefore it is upon the logic rather than upon the crime that you should dwell.

> —"The Adventure of the Copper Beeches,"
> *The Adventures of Sherlock Holmes* (1892)

What it means: *Reason is strong and resilient.*

How to use it: *When representing a criminal defendant, you must move beyond the façade of the crime and try to understand the deep forces at work.*

— *Clue 47* —

Any truth is better than indefinite doubt.

—"The Adventure of the Yellow Face,"
The Memoirs of Sherlock Holmes (1893)

What it means: *Uncertainty is anathema.*

How to use it: *Judges and juries abhor a vacuum, so it's your job to present a clear and convincing solution they can grasp as early in the case as possible.*

— *Clue 48* —

"What the deuce is it to me?" he [Holmes] interrupted impatiently: "You say that we go round the sun. If we went round the moon it would not make a pennyworth of difference to me or to my work."

—*A Study in Scarlet* (1887)

What it means: *Shun the irrelevant.*

How to use it: *In presenting a case to a judge or jury, you must provide them with only the information they need (and no more) in order to make a decision.*

— Clue 49 —

Now is the dramatic moment of fate, Watson, when you hear a step upon the stair which is walking into your life, and you know not whether for good or ill.

—*The Hound of the Baskervilles* (1902)

What it means: *Situations can change quickly and dramatically.*

How to use it: *Learn to accept the volatility of the case and its participants, recognizing that many of these variables are not in your control.*

— *Clue 50* —

As a rule, the more bizarre a thing is the less mysterious it proves to be. It is your commonplace, featureless crimes which are really puzzling, just as a commonplace face is the most difficult to identify.

—"The Adventure of the Red-Headed League,"
The Adventures of Sherlock Holmes (1892)

What it means: *Pedestrian crimes are often the most difficult to defend.*

How to use it: *A criminal attorney soon learns not to be surprised by the challenges of handling a matter that has little to distinguish itself from other crimes.*

— *Clue 51* —

Everything comes in circles. The old wheel turns, and the same
comes up. It's all been done before, and will be again.

—*The Valley of Fear* (1915)

What it means: *Been there, done that.*

How to use it: *A litigator must remember that there are a limited number of ways to
approach a case. Once you have made a decision, don't beat yourself over the head second-
guessing it.*

"My dear Watson," said Sherlock Holmes, "I cannot agree with those who rank modesty among the virtues. To the logician all things should be seen exactly as they are, and to underestimate one's self is as much a departure from truth as to exaggerate one's own powers."

—"The Adventure of the Greek Interpreter,"
The Memoirs of Sherlock Holmes (1893)

What it means: *It is what it is.*

How to use it: *As an attorney you must accept the facts of the case (and your own skills) as they are—good, bad, or indifferent.*

— *Clue 53* —

It was easier to know it than to explain why I know it. If you were asked to prove that two and two made four, you might find some difficulty, and yet you are quite sure of the fact.

—*A Study in Scarlet* (1887)

What it means: *The obvious is often the most difficult to explain.*

How to use it: *As a trial lawyer you must express yourself in a way that leaves absolutely no doubt about your position and how you arrived at it.*

— *Clue 54* —

[Moriarty:] "Everything I have to say has already crossed your mind."
[Holmes:] "Then possibly my answer has crossed yours."

—"A Scandal in Belgravia,"
The Memoirs of Sherlock Holmes (1893)

What it means: *The solution is often right in front of you.*

How to use it: *The key to a litigator's success is typically not the number of facts amassed, but the discernment he uses in dealing with that information.*

— *Clue 55* —

The larger crimes are apt to be the simpler, for the bigger the crime, the more obvious, as a rule, is the motive.

—"A Case of Identity," *The Adventures of Sherlock Holmes* (1892)

What it means: *Smaller crimes can be problematic.*

How to use it: *A criminal lawyer who handles serious matters can usually discern the motive behind the crime, but lesser offenses often present a greater challenge to defend.*

— *Clue 56* —

Anything is better than stagnation.

—"The Adventure of the Sunset Vampire,"
The Case-Book of Sherlock Holmes (1924)

What it means: *Inertia builds interest.*

How to use it: *The worst situation for a litigator is a trial with no real progress, where the wheels spin pointlessly in the sand. As a trial lawyer, you must actively advance the case in order to maintain the attention of the judge and jury.*

— Clue 57 —

Violence does, in truth, recoil upon the violent, and the schemer falls into the pit which he digs for another.

—"The Adventure of the Speckled Band,"
The Adventures of Sherlock Holmes (1892)

What it means: *What goes around, comes around.*

How to use it: *Integrity is essential to the practice of law, and those with few scruples eventually suffer the consequences.*

— Clue 58 —

It is quite a three pipe problem, and I beg that you won't speak to me for
fifty minutes.

—"The Adventure of the Red Headed League,"
The Adventures of Sherlock Holmes (1892)

What it means: *Reflection requires silence.*

How to use it: *A trial lawyer must allow herself plenty of time—without
distractions—to focus on the deeper ramifications and cross-currents of the case at hand.*

— *Clue 59* —

There are times, young fellah, when every one of us must make a stand for human right and justice, or you never feel clean again.

—*The Lost World* (1912)

What it means: *Maintain your self-respect.*

How to use it: *The practice of law is an admirable calling with the opportunity to serve humanity, and those who pursue the profession's highest goals are richly rewarded.*

— *Clue 60* —

When once your point of view is changed, the very thing which was so damning becomes a clue to the truth.

—"The Problem of Thor Bridge,"
The Case-Book of Sherlock Holmes (1922)

What it means: *A change of perspective often allows a solution.*

How to use it: *Never ignore the difficult situation. Try to adjust your thinking to see the issue from a different angle. Like turning the ring on a telephoto lens, the images suddenly click and become clear.*

— *Clue 61* —

"They say that genius is an infinite capacity for taking pains," he [Holmes] remarked with a smile. "It's a very bad definition, but it does apply to detective work."

—*A Study in Scarlet* (1887)

What it means: *Success is spelled h-a-r-d w-o-r-k.*

How to use it: *Take extraordinary measures to represent clients in the courtroom, and you will soon be branded with a reputation for brilliance.*

— *Clue 62* —

Have you tried to drive a harpoon through a body? No? Tut, tut, my dear sir, you must really pay attention to these details.

—"The Adventure of Black Peter,"
The Complete Sherlock Holmes (1905)

What it means: *Neglect the practical at your peril.*

How to use it: *Litigators must test their arguments in the field to make sure they withstand the rigorous testing that extends beyond the academic.*

— Clue 63 —

We must look for consistency. Where there is a want of it we must suspect deception.

—"The Problem of Thor Bridge,"
The Case-Book of Sherlock Holmes (1922)

What it means: *Consistency matters.*

How to use it: *The experienced attorney knows that when there is a break in the narrative, he must pay particular attention to the situation.*

— *Clue 64* —

By a man's finger-nails, by his coat-sleeve, by his boots, by his trouser-knees, by the callosities of his forefinger and thumb, by his expression, by his shirt-cuff—by each of these things a man's calling is plainly revealed. That all united should fail to enlighten the competent inquirer in any case is almost inconceivable. You know that a conjurer gets no credit when once he has explained his trick; and if I show you too much of my method of working, you will come to the conclusion that I am a very ordinary individual after all.

—*A Study in Scarlet* (1887)

What it means: *Careful observation is rare.*

How to use it: *Take the initiative to closely examine all of the facts and applicable law in your case, and you will quickly set yourself apart from your adversaries.*

— Clue 65 —

One's ideas must be as broad as Nature if they are to interpret Nature.

—*A Study in Scarlet* (1887)

What it means: *Use a sufficiently wide angle.*

How to use it: *The failure to view a situation from a high altitude causes you to miss some of the edges around the landscape. This shortcoming can be disastrous in the final analysis.*

— *Clue 66* —

His love of danger, his intense appreciation of the drama of an adventure—all the more intense for being held tightly in—his consistent view that every peril in life is a form of sport, a fierce game betwixt you and Fate, with Death as a forfeit, made him a wonderful companion at such hours.

—*The Lost World* (1912)

What it means: *Appreciate human drama.*

How to use it: *The trial practice is ultimately an adventure that commonly pits individuals against one another in fascinating and unpredictable ways.*

— *Clue 67* —

The chief proof of man's real greatness lies in his perception of his own smallness.

—*The Sign of the Four* (1890)

What it means: *Modesty is key to success.*

How to use it: *Come to grips with the fact that you are human and prone to error, and you will be a far better advocate for it.*

— *Clue 68* —

It is only when a man goes out into the world with the thought that there are heroisms all round him, and with the desire all alive in his heart to follow any which may come within sight of him, that he breaks away from the life he knows, and ventures forth into the wonderful mystic twilight land where lie the great adventures and the great rewards.

—*The Lost World* (1912)

What it means: *Life is an adventure only for the adventurous.*

How to use it: *Carpe diem! Seize the situation before you with enthusiasm, and you will have an impact in the profession that is impossible to achieve without such passion.*

— *Clue 69* —

A fine thought in fine language is a most precious jewel, and should not be hid away, but be exposed for use and ornament.

—*Through the Magic Door* (1907)

What it means: *A thoughtful and well-expressed idea is a thing of beauty.*

How to use it: *As a trial lawyer you should aim for an artful presentation of your client's position. A skillfully worded argument will often prevail over a stronger, but less articulate, position.*

— *Clue 70* —

I should prefer that you do not mention my name at all in connection with this case, as I choose to be only associated with those crimes which present some difficulty in their solution.

—"The Adventure of the Cardboard Box,"
The Memoirs of Sherlock Holmes (1893)

What it means: *Manage your reputation.*

How to use it: *A trial lawyer must craft her image such that she is perceived to be an advocate of some significance. This reputation requires a great deal of cultivation.*

— *Clue 71* —

It is a mistake to confound strangeness with mystery. The most common-place crime is often the most mysterious because it presents no new or special features from which deductions may be drawn. This murder would have been infinitely more difficult to unravel had the body of the victim been simply found lying in the roadway without any of those outré and sensational accompaniments which have rendered it remarkable. These strange details, far from making the case more difficult, have really had the effect of making it less so.

—*A Study in Scarlet* (1887)

What it means: *Common crimes are often the most difficult.*

How to use it: *A criminal lawyer is involved in an irony of sorts: the stranger the crime, the easier it may be to defend.*

— *Clue 72* —

For strange effects and extraordinary combinations we must go to life itself, which is always far more daring than any effort of the imagination.

—"The Adventure of the Red-Headed League,"
The Adventures of Sherlock Holmes (1892)

What it means: *Truth is more challenging than fiction.*

How to use it: *A trial lawyer must learn to accept the limits of imagination. Reality, with its limitless permutations, is far more challenging.*

— *Clue 73* —

He was too absurd to make me angry. Indeed, it was a waste of energy, for if you were going to be angry with this man you would be angry all the time.

—*The Lost World* (1912)

What it means: *Avoid being ruffled by the antics of others.*

How to use it: *Never let opposing counsel—no matter how difficult or unreasonable— get under your skin. Such distractions only interfere with your objectivity, which is absolutely essential to representing your client.*

He has a gentle voice and a quiet manner, but behind his twinkling blue eyes there lurks a capacity for furious wrath and implacable resolution, the more dangerous because they are held in leash.

—*The Lost World* (1912)

74

What it means: *The most unlikely individuals can turn violent.*

How to use it: *A lawyer must watch closely for the unpredictable behavior of others. A repressed individual can suddenly display erratic behavior that is completely at odds with his outward persona.*

— *Clue 75* —

There are strange red depths in the soul of the most commonplace man.

—*The Lost World* (1912)

What it means: *The capacity for evil should never be underestimated.*

How to use it: *Some of the greatest atrocities are committed by the least likely suspects, and the lawyer should never be alarmed.*

— *Clue 76* —

How small we feel with our petty ambitions and strivings in the presence of the great elemental forces of Nature!

—*The Sign of the Four* (1890)

What it means: *Maintain perspective.*

How to use it: *An attorney, no matter how brilliant, must remain modest, or she will be swept away in an egotism that is detrimental to her and to her client.*

— *Clue 77* —

"Winwood Reade is good upon the subject," said Holmes. "He remarks that, while the individual man is an insoluble puzzle, in the aggregate he becomes a mathematical certainty. You can, for example, never foretell what any one man will do, but you can say with precision what an average number will be up to. Individuals vary, but percentages remain constant. So says the statistician."

—*The Sign of the Four* (1890)

What it means: *Generalizations are useful in framing legal issues.*

How to use it: *The attorney must understand that statistics may be helpful in the general analysis of a situation, but there are always individuals and situations that do not fit the norm.*

— *Clue 78* —

It is not really difficult to construct a series of inferences, each dependent upon its predecessor and each simple in itself. If, after doing so, one simply knocks out all the central inferences and presents one's audience with the starting-point and the conclusion, one may produce a startling, though perhaps a meretricious, effect.

—"The Adventure of the Dancing Men,"
The Return of Sherlock Holmes (1905)

What it means: *Things are often not as they appear.*

How to use it: *Legal arguments are frequently built on suppositions that change, which leads to a sequence of events different from what was originally anticipated. Your job as an advocate is to show the reasonableness of the relief sought in light of the facts proven.*

Sherlock Holmes closed his eyes and placed his elbows upon the arms of his chair, with his finger-tips together. "The ideal reasoner," he remarked, "would, when he had once been shown a single fact in all its bearings, deduce from it not only all the chain of events which led up to it but also all the results which would follow from it. As Cuvier could correctly describe a whole animal by the contemplation of a single bone, so the observer who has thoroughly understood one link in a series of incidents should be able to accurately state all the other ones, both before and after. We have not yet grasped the results which the reason alone can attain to."

79

—"The Five Orange Pips,"
The Adventures of Sherlock Holmes (1892)

What it means: *Knowledge and experience are essential to professional success.*

How to use it: *An attorney must utilize both his educational and his practical skills in order to best serve his client. One without the other is far less effective.*

— *Clue 80* —

I examine the data, as an expert, and pronounce a specialist's opinion. I claim no credit in such cases. My name figures in no newspaper. The work itself, the pleasure of finding a field for my peculiar powers, is my highest reward.

—*The Sign of the Four* (1890)

What it means: *Work is its own reward.*

How to use it: *A true professional excels for the sake of her craft, not for the applause of others.*

— *Clue 81* —

A man should keep his little brain attic stocked with all the furniture that he is likely to use, and the rest he can put away in the lumber-room of his library where he can get it if he wants it.

—"The Five Orange Pips,"
The Adventures of Sherlock Holmes (1892)

What it means: *Be discriminatory.*

How to use it: *Know what information you need to have at your fingertips and that which you can store and retrieve later.*

— *Clue 82* —

The more outre and grotesque an incident is the more carefully it deserves to be examined, and the very point which appears to complicate a case is, when duly considered and scientifically handled, the one which is most likely to elucidate it.

—*The Hound of the Baskervilles* (1902)

82

What it means: *Complications frequently bring resolution.*

How to use it: *A lawyer must thoroughly consider the difficulties of a case, confident that the solution often lies therein.*

Problems may be solved in the study which have baffled all those who have sought a solution by the aid of their senses. To carry the art, however, to its highest pitch, it is necessary that the reasoner should be able to utilize all the facts which have come to his knowledge; and this in itself implies, as you will readily see, a possession of all knowledge, which, even in these days of free education and encyclopedias, is a somewhat rare accomplishment. It is not so impossible, however, that a man should possess all knowledge which is likely to be useful to him in his work, and this I have endeavored in my case to do.

—"The Five Orange Pips,"
The Adventures of Sherlock Holmes (1892)

What it means: *A rigorous mental analysis trumps all others.*

How to use it: *Use your mind to solve your client's problems. Decisions made without deep thought prove far less fruitful.*

— *Clue 84* —

Never trust to general impressions, my boy, but concentrate yourself upon details. My first glance is always at a woman's sleeve. In a man, it is perhaps better to take the knee of the trouser. Chance has put in our way a most singular and whimsical problem, and its solution is its own reward.

—"The Adventure of the Blue Carbuncle,"
The Adventures of Sherlock Holmes (1892)

What it means: Connections between events are critical.

How to use it: Examining the details closely, with an eye for cause and effect, pays handsome rewards.

— *Clue 85* —

I have already explained to you that what is out of the common is usually a guide rather than a hindrance. In solving a problem of this sort, the grand thing is to be able to reason backwards. That is a very useful accomplishment, and a very easy one, but people do not practice it much. In the every-day affairs of life it is more useful to reason forwards, and so the other comes to be neglected. There are fifty who can reason synthetically for one who can reason analytically.

—*A Study in Scarlet* (1887)

What it means: *Reverse logic is useful.*

How to use it: *A lawyer must be able to take a situation and trace possible developments back in time.*

— *Clue 86* —

The difficulty is to detach the framework of fact—of absolute undeniable fact—from the embellishments of theorists and reporters.

—"Silver Blaze," *The Memoirs of Sherlock Holmes* (1893)

What it means: *Prune ruthlessly.*

How to use it: *The ability to distinguish fact from fancy is invaluable for lawyers who are serious about analyzing their cases.*

— Clue 87 —

See the value of imagination. It is the one quality which Inspector Gregory lacks. We imagined what might have happened, acted upon the supposition, and find ourselves justified. Let us proceed.

—"Silver Blaze," *The Memoirs of Sherlock Holmes* (1893)

What it means: *Think outside the box.*

How to use it: *A litigator must approach a case creatively in order to arrive at the best solution.*

I have heard your reasons and regard them as unconvincing and inadequate.

—"The Adventure of the Devil's Foot," *His Last Bow* (1910)

What it means: *Critique the argument.*

How to use it: *To improve, a trial lawyer must never resist candid criticism of her arguments and presentation skills.*

— *Clue 89* —

Most people, if you describe a train of events to them will tell you what the result would be. They can put those events together in their minds, and argue from them that something will come to pass. There are few people, however, who, if you told them a result, would be able to evolve from their own inner consciousness what the steps were which led up to that result. This power is what I mean when I talk of reasoning backward, or analytically.

—*A Study in Scarlet* (1887)

What it means: *Reason from the end to the beginning.*

How to use it: *An attorney must learn to view legal problems in an analytical fashion that allows him to discern the events that led to the controversy.*

— *Clue 90* —

It was a net from which it seemed to me, a few hours ago, that there was no possible escape. But he had not that supreme gift of the artist, the knowledge of when to stop. He wished to improve that which was already perfect and so he ruined all.

—"The Adventure of the Norwood Builder,"
The Return of Sherlock Holmes (1905)

What it means: *Know when to stop.*

How to use it: *A litigator must know when to finish her presentation to the judge or jury. Going beyond that point has destroyed many a fine argument.*

— *Clue 91* —

Yet birth, and lust, and illness, and death are changeless things, and when one of these harsh facts springs out upon a man at some sudden turn of the path of life, it dashes off for the moment his mask of civilization and gives a glimpse of the stranger and stronger face below.

—"The Curse of Eve," *Round the Red Lamp* (1894)

What it means: *Adversity is revealing.*

How to use it: *A structural engineer quickly realizes that placing stress on metal reveals it faults, and an attorney must learn to do likewise in the preparation of his cases.*

"And a singularly consistent investigation you have made, my dear Watson," said he. "I cannot at the moment recall any possible blunder which you have omitted. The total effect of your proceeding has been to give the alarm everywhere and yet to discover nothing."

—"The Disappearance of Lady Frances Carfax,"
His Last Bow (1911)

What it means: Choose substance over form.

How to use it: Make sure that your efforts in presenting the case to the judge or jury are producing real results.

— *Clue 93* —

My line of thoughts about dogs is analogous. A dog reflects the family life. Whoever saw a frisky dog in a gloomy family, or a sad dog in a happy one? Snarling people have snarling dogs, dangerous people have dangerous ones. And their passing moods may reflect the passing moods of others.

—"The Adventure of the Creeping Man,"
The Case-Book of Sherlock Holmes (1927)

What it means: *Pay close attention to an individual's surroundings.*

How to use it: *To understand the complexities of the case, you must observe all the circumstances affecting the person or situation under examination.*

— *Clue 94* —

I knew you came from Afghanistan. . . . The train of reasoning ran, "Here is a gentleman of a medical type, but with the air of a military man. Clearly an army doctor, then. He has just come from the tropics, for his face is dark, and that is not the natural tint of his skin, for his wrists are fair. He has undergone hardship and sickness, as his haggard face says clearly. His left arm has been injured. He holds it in a stiff and unnatural manner. Where in the tropics could an English army doctor have seen much hardship and got his arm wounded? Clearly in Afghanistan."

—*A Study in Scarlet* (1887)

What it means: *Closely observe, and then carefully deduce.*

How to use it: *A lawyer who makes a habit of paying keen attention to the details of her case will excel in her service to the client.*

[Lord St. Simon:] "I understand that you have already managed several delicate cases of this sort, sir, though I presume that they were hardly from the same class of society."

[Holmes:] "My last client of the sort was a King."

[Lord St. Simon:] "What! Had he lost his wife?"

[Holmes:] "You can understand," said Holmes suavely, "that I extend to the affairs of my other clients the same secrecy which I promise to you in yours."

—"The Adventure the Noble Batchelor,"
The Adventures of Sherlock Holmes (1892)

What it means: *Maintain client confidences.*

How to use it: *A professional never breaches the confidence of a client, no matter how seemingly insignificant. That which a client shares with you is presumed to be private unless the client explicitly instructs otherwise.*

The work is its own reward.

—"The Adventure of the Norwood Builder,"
The Return of Sherlock Holmes (1905)

What it means: A profession is a calling.

How to use it: The practice of law at its highest levels is more than a mere occupation, and the attorney must always keep in mind its high ideals as he represents his clients.

— *Clue 97* —

Perhaps when a man has special knowledge and special powers like my own, it often rather encourages him to seek a complex explanation when a simpler one is at hand.

> —"The Adventure of the Abbey Grange,"
> *The Return of Sherlock Holmes* (1905)

What it means: *Seek the simple.*

How to use it: *A lawyer should avoid a complicated solution to a problem when a simple one will do.*

— *Clue 98* —

If it should ever strike you that I am getting a little over-confident in my powers, or giving less pains to a case than it deserves, kindly whisper "Norbury" in my ear, and I shall be infinitely obliged to you.

—"The Adventure of the Yellow Face,"
The Memoirs of Sherlock Holmes (1893)

What it means: *Avoid overconfidence and laziness.*

How to use it: *Modesty and diligence, ironically enough, are the keys to a lawyer's success.*

It is a singular thing, but I find that a concentrated atmosphere helps a concentration of thought. I have not pushed it to the limit of getting into a box to think, but that is the logical outcome of my convictions.

—*The Hound of the Baskervilles* (1902)

What it means: *Think without distraction.*

How to use it: *The more intensely you can analyze a case in isolation, the better decision you will render to your client.*

— *Clue 100* —

I am the last and highest court of appeal in detection.

—*The Sign of the Four* (1890)

What it means: *Maintain your sense of humor.*

How to use it: *A tongue-in-cheek approach to the practice of law often introduces a much-needed sense of levity.*

About the Author

Cecil C. Kuhne III is a litigator in the Dallas office of Norton Rose Fulbright US L.L.P.